SHE TOO
FOUR VOICES IN (ALMOST) HARMONY

Delaina J. Miller
Rosemary Nissen-Wade
Helen Patrice
Leigh D.C. Spencer

She Too: Four Voice in (Almost) Harmony © 2025 by Delaina J. Miller, Rosemary Nissen-Wade, Helen Patrice, and Leigh D.C. Spencer

Published by Content X Design, Inc.
Overland Park, KS
contentxdesign.com

All rights reserved.

Second Edition
First published by Content X Design in 2014

Cover art: Sisters of the Storm by Jeanie Tomanek
Venn diagram: Bill Seney
Cover design: Allison Pang
Book design: Allison Pang
Editor: Carina Bissett

Printed in the United States of America
ISBN: 978-1-942005-68-1
Library of Congress Control Number: 2025930722

Also by Delaina J. Miller, Rosemary Nissen-Wade, Helen Patrice, and Leigh D.C. Spencer

Paper Birds

In the Beginning

Delaina   **Leigh**   **Rosemary**   **Helen**

1988

D   L   R   H

2008

D   L   R   H

2009

D   L   R   H

2010

D   L   R   H

2011

L   R   D   H

Foreword

What is it that calls poets to gather? The wind, the moon, a charm for summoning a witch? In the case of the women who came together a decade ago to create this book, it was all of these things and more. For powerful magic requires the right ingredients, collected organically through shared interests and joyous discoveries. Sure, these things take time. But what is time to a poet other than a string of moments captured on paper by pen?

The first edition of *She Too: Four Voices in (Almost) Harmony* was published in 2014 as a collaborative project created by Delaina J. Miller, Rosemary Nissen-Wade, Helen Patrice, and Leigh D.C. Spencer. Each day during the month of April (National Poetry Month in the United States), these poets joined countless others in taking inspiration from daily prompts offered by Robert Lee Brewer at the Poem A Day (PAD) challenge at *Writer's Digest*, and NaPoWriMo, an independent project created by Maine poet Maureen Thorson. The end result was the lovely collection you hold in your hands, a collection of poems that weaves through the lives of four women living on opposite ends of the world.

When it was first published, *She Too: Four Voices in (Almost) Harmony* instantly garnered attention and critical acclaim. Michele Brenton, author of the bestselling poetry culture parody *Fifty Shades of Blue*, called it "A fascinating view into four poetic worlds which share points of contact while remaining decisively and endearingly individual." Karin Gustafson, author of *Going on Somewhere*, also noted the way the work by these four poets spoke to each other: "[The] spirit of shared celebration, concentrated exploration, and disciplined flow resonate in unwinding narratives that both amuse and enlighten." But none of this would have been possible without a few magical, chance encounters along the way.

It all started in 1988, when Helen found the inspiration to write Rosemary a fan letter. The two, who both lived in Australia, met in person and began what has become a life-long friendship. Fast forward ten years to the first meeting of Delaina and Leigh through the shared love of knowledge and women's studies at the University of Arizona. The two U.S. poets bonded over potato tacos and bean burritos and have stayed in touch ever since. In 2009, Rosemary and Leigh connected across the ocean through a poetry page on Facebook. And then, over the next two years, Helen and Delaina joined them in this cyber space, forming the Brave Hearts chat group, where they encouraged each other to spread their roots, grow new branches, and reach for the sun.

It was only natural that they would later make a promise to each other to write a poem a month during the month of April. Afterward, they celebrated by collecting their work into a book they could share with others. And even though the poems in this book cover a wide range of subjects, they speak to each other in interesting and often unexpected ways.

In "Ready to Go," Leigh D.C. Spencer reminisces on Sunday dinners before technology forever changed the way families spend time together. Rosemary Nissen-Wade takes it a step further with a metaphorical contemplation on the Internet's influence on the evolution of poetry—from straw to wood to metal to cyberspace—in "The Last Straw Poem." The moon, too, becomes common ground for poetic exploration. Delaina J. Miller provides a safe space for secrets and companionship during dark times in her gentle offering "If I Were the Moon." In sharp contrast, Helen Patrice explores the passion of wild nights under the full moon in "Call of the Hunt." The poems communicate with one another much like the mysterious mycelium that reaches through the soil to connect trees on opposite ends of the forest. There is magic in that. The treble of timber attuned to the seasons. The melody of leaves rattling in the breeze. Four voices coming together in a song of their own making.

As in the sequel *Paper Birds*, each poet's voice has been preserved in regard to regional differences. For instance, when it comes to spelling and grammar, both Rosemary and Helen write using British English, whereas Delaina and Leigh rely on American English conventions. Minor edits have been made in this anniversary edition of *She Too: Four Voices in (Almost) Harmony* but, as a whole, this book stands the test of time.

In these pages, you will catch glimpses of these poets—their experiences and emotions in the present as well as their reflections on the past and their hopes for the future. You'll discover the joy of walking dragons, an ode to a misfit monster, the power of saying no on a bad first date, and the joyous flight to a marriage once forbidden.

Ten years later, and these women are still writing and cheering each other on. This continuing call to create is brilliantly framed in Rosemary Nissen-Wade's "Future Poem":

> Look up ahead – do you see
> the future poem beckoning?
> Your present poems are merely steps on the way.

And it seems she was right, as evidenced by their second collaboration in *Paper Birds*. From the roots these women have planted over the years to the birds they shelter in their branches, these four poets have created their own ecosystem based on friendship and the power of words. So, I urge you now, step into the woods. A magical journey awaits.

—Carina Bissett, award-winning editor, author, and poet

Dedication:

To Andrew, Bill, Earl, and Kristin
who have always put up with our poetic madness
and even inspire some of it.

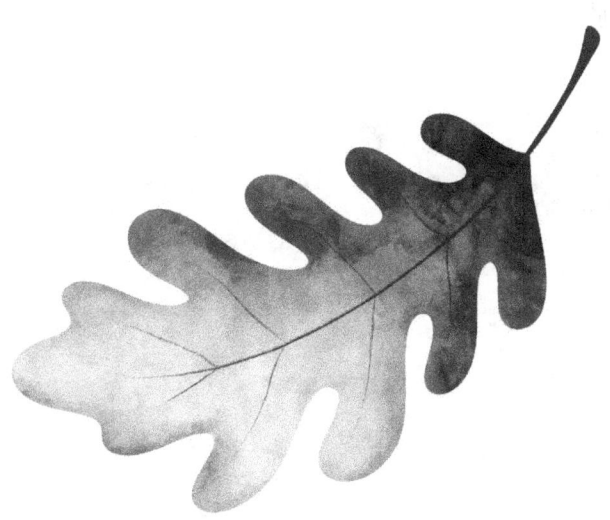

Contents

A 'Mystical Dragon'	1
The Discovery of Light	2
A Place of Meditation	4
Midnight Blue	5
Family Tree	6
Peace Is	8
In the Cauldron of Love	9
Red	10
Call of the Hunt	12
If I Were the Moon	14
Watching the Pendulum	15
Shelter from the Storm	16
If I Were Brave	17
Last Night in Cusco	18
Charm for Summoning a Witch	21
Tell It to the Wind	22
Found	24
Endings and Beginnings	26
Earth Half Full	28
Tomorrow	29
Walking with Dragons	30
Feline	32
Rexy, the Killer Chihuahua	33
Apple	34
The Cat's Out of the Bag	36
New Neighbors	38
Not Fulfilling Their Obligations: A Partially Found Poem	39
An Owl in Love with a Deer	40
Why Be the Cow?	42
My Last Duchess	46

Favorite Monster	48
Things That Go Bump	50
Into the Mind of an Alien	52
Launching Magic	53
Since You Asked	54
A Text From My Soul	56
The Basics	58
The Meanest Things	60
First Date	62
Tell It to the Empty Chair	64
Lazarus' Jewel Box	66
Trying on Clothes	67
Attic	68
Cold Water	70
The Newer Habitat	71
Waterfall	72
Storms	73
Weather Report, Ouside and In	74
The Question of Safety	76
The Last Straw	77
Happy Easter	78
Before It Is Too Late	80
The Poet Dreams of Dreams	81
Since You Left	82
The Grim	84
Arranging After-Care	85
Remembering the Dead	86
Anti-Elegy	88
You Heard He Was Dead	89
The Monster Collective	90
The Death of Poverty	94
How I Miss Those Years	95
Strength Discovered	96
The Traveller	99
Passage	100
Solo in San Francisco	101
When I Went Back to Melbourne	104
Dirt Roads and Forgotten Highways	106

Camping in the Rain	108
City of Fountains	111
Colour	112
She Is	114
Unstill Life	116
A Photomontage of Me	118
Passion, Madness, Orchids	120
A Picture Paints a Thousand Words	121
If I were Writing in Sanskrit	122
Ready to Go	123
The Last Straw Poem	126
In Kitchens All Over Suburbia	128
Cinquain for Phillip	129
Meeting in Coles	130
Sweetness Settled	132
Night Poem	134
The Secret's in the Sauce	136
That Smell	138
Peanut Butter and Jelly	140
Starts	142
Elegy for DeAnza	143
Baby Longs to Be Admiral	146
Alternate Realities	147
My Knight Teddy Bear PJs	148
Pop Culture on Loan	149
War Games	150
Optimist and Pessimist Attend a Fundraiser	152
Signs of the Future	153
Comforting Myself	154
Safe Havens	155
Doing the Usual	156
Family Quilt	158
Note to Self	160
Tell It to the Lips	161
Bitter Love Poem	162
Home	164
Early Morning	166
Love Song to an Amino Acid	167

I Love	168
If I Were a Love Poem	170
Unveiling	171
Since I Said Yes	174
White Anglo-Saxon Love	175
Settled	176
River Ends	178
Calling It a Day	179
Future Poem	181
Finished!	183
The Prompts that Started It All	185
Acknowledgements	189
About the Poet: Delaina J. Miller	190
About the Poet: Rosemary Nissen-Wade	191
About the Poet: Helen Patrice	192
About the Poet: Leigh D.C. Spencer	193

At 'Mystical Dragon'

Helen Patrice

In the purple room we
search for the real beyond the real,
as summer slides down into cool.

In the purple room we
journey to lives we have left
behind, in this psychic school.

In the purple room we
hear, with no ears, angels sing,
know there is no such thing as sin.

In the purple room we
pace, find curtains thin,
as we walk realms of ghost and djinn.

In the purple room we
smell incense drifting like jazz
on warm air that belies winter June.

In the purple room we
know that to die
is to transform.

We will emerge butterflies soon
enough.

The Discovery of Light

Rosemary Nissen-Wade

Light, light, so much light!
Suddenly, at the end of the slow process,
enormous brightness everywhere.
And everywhere became larger.

I didn't have words, and scarcely thought.
But I had perception. I perceived
bedazzlement and my body's reaction.
Now I would call it shock.

Noise, too, was everywhere, huge,
around and through me. I had, you see,
no sense of a separate self. I
was the everywhere, with no edges.

I began to distinguish voices.
'She', they kept repeating, and somehow
I knew that 'She' was me. So began
the experience of limits.

In every direction, whiteness – which had
angles and corners. Heads and bodies
disappeared behind what I now see as walls;
but then I had no names, no concepts.

Movement was happening. Noses and chins,
cheeks and mouths and eyes, which I did not then
know or understand, moved close and away.
There was a sense of speed, of bustling.

And I felt myself moved (not fast, not a lot).
I was taken and wrapped, moved further from
a part of the everything, a dim lump
that I knew I needed – my exhausted mother.

And all the time, startled by light. I kept looking.
I began to experience my mind's reaction too,
which now I identify as awakening
curiosity, even a beginning of wonder.

A Place of Meditation

Delaina J. Miller

Deep breath in—I am
long exhale—Love

> in—I am
> out—Love
>
> in—silence
> out—thought
>
> in the moment
> out amid the universe
>
> in discovery—I am
> out to the world—me
>
> in a state of being
> outside limitations
>
> in my head dancing with light
> outward my heart offers warmth

in breath, I exist
out of vapor, I expand.

Midnight Blue

Delaina J. Miller

A pearl suspended
in midnight blue.
A whisper
a glimmer
embodied in Love's universe.

Family Tree

Leigh D.C. Spencer

One side
blossoms

Fruit and shade
enough for everyone

Roots

For sitting
contemplating
meditating

The other side
bitter

Black and barren

Roots

Crumble
give way
for splinters
and dark thoughts

Equal care yields
equal gifts
in accordance with the true nature
of each side

I cannot deny
I am of one whole tree

Not always belonging
on the side of light and spring

Finding occasional comfort
in the gnarling dark

Peace Is

Rosemary Nissen-Wade

The fed infant falling asleep
in the crook of your cradling arm.

The cat beside you on the bed,
purring all night long.

As you meditate in your back yard,
songs of small birds in the trees.

The face of a beloved friend
smiling to see you again.

Standing under a warm shower
as the water runs over your shoulders.

Arriving home on a cold night,
coming in and closing the door.

In The Cauldron of Love

Helen Patrice

As the Sun lowers his gaze,
last fierceness grimacing the sky red,
Pele dances in her red skirts.
On billows of steam,
She rises.
She of the glowing eyes,
She of the flowing black hair,
She of passion, She of the birth of land.
Her sparks dance in the air.
Watch too long and feel Her call.
Descend into Her caldera,
become one with Her earth,
melt to the core.
Her fire is red as blood,
and to love Her is to burn.
Lay your heart on a ti leaf,
and give it to Her.

Red

Leigh D.C. Spencer

Cowering
like shy Gollum
in the corner
of the thrift shop dressing room

I never

would have even tried
the little dress on

But she made me

I don't mean that as
a figurative excuse

My cheerful friend
and shopping companion
shoved the dress into my arms

Lovingly

Saying
"Just shut up and put it on!"

Impossible challenge one—complete
It actually zipped

Impossible challenge two—pending
Actually stepping out of the dressing room

A total stranger told me I looked stunning

But

She didn't scrutinize
the visible flabby underparts of my arms
when I wave them
like I'm dancing
or having a seizure
like I did
My friend snapped a picture with her phone
to send to my husband

He approved
by way of the
wonderfully vulgar comments
I married him for

So I bought the dress

Hoping three weeks was enough time
to find the perfect accessory

Courage
to actually wear it

It was strapless

It was sparkly

It was red

Call of the Hunt

Helen Patrice

Hounds baying from a distance, drawing closer.
She kisses her husband, but must go.
The peace of home,
the quiet songs sung to children before bed
forgotten.
There is no cure for this love of the Goddess.
She is wife and mother,
but also of people,
women,
who run to the Moon.
Out the door into wild night.
She is barefoot, naked,
and this love is ferocious and wild.
She joins the Hunt
across fields and towards the hills.
Faster, as civilisation tears away.
The heights, the heights!
With the others, she screams,
chants from an ancient language.
Amongst them, a shining woman,
running easily, calling her dogs.
They reach the summit,
and She is gone from them,
ascended along moonbeams.
The women fall, spent,
crying to Her:

'Take me with you!'
They sleep in the Moon's light
and tomorrow will go back
to house, well water,
the hard work of living.
Tonight is theirs,
and this greater love.

If I Were the Moon

Delaina J. Miller

I would hear the whispers of lovers
and keep secrets safe.

I would light up the stars,
so the lost would never lose their place.

I would comfort the lonely
with moonbeams dancing through trees.

Absolute darkness would not blind
the heart to beauty yet to be seen.

I would hold the tide
before I let you drown.

I would light a path throughout the night,
so answers to prayers could be found.

I would inspire your dreams
then give you the sun.

Watching The Pendulum

Helen Patrice

The metal chain looped over my fingers.
The brass plumb-bob swinging.
My mouth dry,
tongue hard against my palate,
tasting bitter after green tea.
Soaring voice and violin playing
in the background.
The room full of female voices,
asking questions of their wise-woman selves.
The pendulum circles:
       no.
The pendulum swings:
       yes.
Senses dropping away.
There is only this,
and what my wise woman knows.

Shelter from the Storm

Rosemary Nissen-Wade

A rain day, one
I watch from indoors
though later I must go out.

Last night I called dragons
into the temple – four,
one to each quarter.

Breathing together
in circle, we women
built a pillar of light.

My friend goes home
to sell her house and move
because the floods are coming.

My little cats love storms
and gaze from the top step
under the porch roof.

If I were Brave

Leigh D.C. Spencer

If I were brave
I would feel the wind in my hair

Watch the ground
leave my feet
Soaring

Higher
Faster
Freer

As a bird
recognizing only the beauty of flight
with no thought of the destination

Or the crash

I am not capable
of such leaps of faith

But I take one step

Then another

So perhaps
I am brave
enough

Last Night in Cusco

Rosemary Nissen-Wade

We waited for Wendy in her hotel foyer. It was an old hotel, just off the city centre – cool stone walls; plants on balconies; polished tables; graceful stairs. I tried on the coneshaped black felt hat I bought at the market – not the tourist market; the people's market where Wendy took us, down near the station. As soon as I put the hat on, I saw pulsing flashes of light all around the walls and the high ceiling. I took it off. The lights vanished.

a slender woman
walks up a slender staircase
tall green plants in tubs

Wendy arrived, all in black as always, with her own hat of high white straw, wide-brimmed, and her big smile. We were to meet three of her Peruvian friends. Just as they arrived, she received a message. The president's daughter was ready to take her to meet the president. Wendy's mission in Peru was to set up shelters and trade schools for homeless kids. She couldn't miss this opportunity. A brief apology, and she left us with her friends. She introduced them by name, but always spoke of them collectively as the Angels. They were a thin young man and two women: one young, shy, quietly pretty; the other older, full-figured, dignified.

she dresses in black
with intent: the uniform
of the grandmothers

The Angels wanted to meet us because we were Reiki Masters. A man had come to Cusco only a few weeks before, and taught them hands-on healing. They were still thrilled, and wanted to compare. After a quick discussion with each other in Spanish, they took us to the young man's home, in a tiny old car that chugged alarmingly up the steep streets. We piled out at a high, blank wall. He opened a small door in the bottom right corner. We bent our heads to go through to a courtyard. Doors around all the inner walls. One was his; he let us into two dark rooms with weak overhead lamps.

rooms without windows
the blue of the Cusco sky
is legendary

They told us about their way of healing. 'We pray', they said, 'And light comes into our hands. May we show you?' We stood in a circle. The older woman prayed in Spanish. I don't know what she said. We had no Spanish much, beyond 'Hola!' When she finished, she invited us to look at their hands, at little sparks of light dancing all over the palms. Then we all noticed Andrew's and my hands sparkling too. Everyone got very excited, pointing and gabbling.

she stands in prayer
her speaking voice is music
on our last night here

They told us the light was a gift from the angels. I asked if the angels could explain what happened when I put on the black felt hat. She took the hat in her hands and closed her eyes. At length she told me it had belonged to a humble shepherd who prayed a lot to Jesus. She said I could summon Jesus whenever I put on the hat; it was full of blessings because of the goodness of that humble man. I supposed that the light-giving angels told her this, into her mind, while she stood with her eyes closed.

We felt nothing, no sensation, but the sparks of light continued for hours until gradually slowing, fading. We left Cusco next day. We never found out what words were used in the prayer.

in a small dark room
we meet with angels of light
farewell to Peru

Charm for Summoning A Witch

Helen Patrice

First off, chocolate, great big blocks,
wild green garden, woolly socks.
A small black cat with a cheeky face,
a floaty dress with ribbons and lace.
Pointy hat, just for fun,
wildlife galore, coloured and dun.
Ink and poetry, books and books,
Ravens, crows, jackdaws, rooks.
Feathers, sparkles, cauldron, candle,
all the elements she can handle.
Mix together, still not enough.
She's virgin, mother, wise and tough.

Tell It to the Wind

Rosemary Nissen-Wade

'Tell it to the wind', said Ramtha*
'And I will hear you, I'll be there'.

I used to do that sometimes
when I lived out under a big sky –
that wide swirling-space for the wind,
and the vast expanse of stars
far away from the blinding
lights of cities.

Always
I felt his presence in response.

That was a long time ago,
though it seems so fresh.
Even in this little rural town
the street lights are shining,
and the sky between the mountains
is often overcast, windless.

Somewhere along the way
I almost forgot Ramtha.

I don't remember why
I spoke to him in the wind –
what I wanted to say,
what I thought he might reply –
but I was lonely then,
at the silent end of my second marriage.

Widowed after my long and happy third,
I do miss someone to talk things over with ...

Ramtha. A channelled being who came to prominence in the eighties.

Found

Delaina J. Miller

It was hanging about
for anyone to see
but no one seemed to notice
it was even there.

Despite the chatter
and the sonnets,
sentiments arrive mute
to deaf ears.

Until a hand stretches out
with fingers firm to take hold
pulling the fallen to their feet.
Or hands like open nets to break the fall.

A handshake, the touch
enough to fill a spirit with hope,
adds some bills to an empty palm.
Watch the wealth roll in.

A kiss upon a scraped knee,
a hug sheltering a wounded heart,
a cool cloth placed upon the bruised,
the battered but not beaten.

Once its discovery was made
it could be seen everywhere
by those who took the time to see
past the hate, past the fear

to the light that burns so bright
in our eyes. The passion to survive
is the same we give each other to thrive.
The discovery that love is healthy and alive.

Endings and Beginnings

Rosemary Nissen-Wade

Morning in the Caldera
is mist and warbling magpies
this time of year,
as summer softens to autumn.

The mountains are clear;
you can see every detail,
and there's just a slight coolness
in the early, after-dawn air.

I go out into the advancing day,
meet an old friend and a new.
One, custodian of ancient land,
will leave it as the other comes in.

One opened portals, sank a bore,
kept the ground chemical-free.
The other plans to create a peace farm
to teach adults and nurture children.

When the day began, I did not know
the Universe would use me this way
to connect these two, who until today
knew nothing at all of each other.

By day's end I am home alone,
a good day's work done.
Coolness returns as the sun falls
gradually down past the horizon.

I watch our mountains turn darker blue,
and say my prayers of gratitude.
I too was a guardian of that land, briefly.
This transfer of energy matters deeply.

Earth Half Full

Delaina J. Miller

Signs of winter almost gone,
trees no longer completely bare.
Buds and blooms dot the space
between branch and earth,
as Nature watercolors
here and there.

White with pink frills
on a dogwood bloom
next to the magnolia tree.
Tulips bright yellow, orange,
and purple deep with the beauty
of the night.

A splash
of optimistic delight
comes to life
on this, only slightly chilly,
Earth Day night.

Tomorrow

Leigh D.C. Spencer

Tomorrow is my favorite day!

It's the one where
EVERYTHING
gets done

Laundry
Yard work
Dishes
Painting the bathroom
Finishing that novel
Putting all those pictures into frames
Making that gourmet seven-course meal
in a spotless kitchen

Was ever a day more hopeful
and productive
than tomorrow?

Waking with Dragons

Leigh D.C. Spencer

My eyes are not open
yet I feel their presence

Stalking

Curious and tentative
at first
becoming more aggressive

Insistent

There are at least two
maybe three

I feel a claw on bare skin
leg poking out from the blanket
as the smallest begins its ascent

Do they sense that I am waking?
That the time of offering is near?

Flanked at one side, the largest
weight on my chest now

Hot breath
panting anticipation

I open a tentative eye
inviting no fire

But a wash of kisses
and happy yelps

My dog dragons
of nine, twelve and forty pounds
delight at my waking

Their primeval stealth rewarded
with offerings of head pats
belly scratches
and breakfast

Feline

Rosemary Nissen-Wade

In the dim light
he is hard to see,
the tawny tiger
resting in the height
of the shadowy green
in the sly dark.

Though his face is dark,
his eyes gleam light
not yellow but green,
and I know he can see
where I try to hide,
my fabulous tiger.

And I can see, against the green
of the bedroom chair in which he hides,
my cat in the dark with eyes of light.

Rexy, The Killer Chihuahua

Helen Patrice

The dog goes crazy at the door,
barking every bark in his head,
as he scrabbles across the floor.

The plumber to fix the heating, which is dead,
ignores the thrashing beast.
Tiny white pup with no street cred.

The dog wishes for a feast
of evil visitors
rolled in carrot, cheese, and yeast.

He defends, protects, loves us
as much as his voice and heart can stand,
with every fibre of him ready to fuss.

Apple
(Ode to a Shelter Dog)

Leigh D.C. Spencer

Her intake picture looked pathetic—old stray dog
Fat chiweenie girl was meant to be someone's companion
So we drove an hour to the shelter
To be sure her hope wasn't lost
Tested her spirit with our whole family
Appreciation shone in her cloudy old eyes

Cataracts also shone in those sweet eyes
This was a fat, lumpy, very old dog
With manners that say she came from a family
Tail wagging, child following, happy little companion
How on earth was she lost?
Picked up as a stray and dumped at the shelter?

Is a cage with food and a cold, wet concrete floor really shelter?
Strange noises and smells make fear visible, even through blind eyes
Love, warmth, security, her life before—lost
But her tail never stops wagging, silly hopeful dog
She's still an enthusiastic companion
Just waiting for her chance to show a new family

I have to wonder, sweet as she is, about her family
How they let her end up here, a death row dog, at the shelter
So gentle, she immediately chose the spastic four year old as her companion
Before age clouded them, did she look lovingly upon a similar child with those kind eyes?
She's a tolerant, non-growling, mellow gem, this dog
Did they even look for her when they discovered what they lost?

Maybe the puppy glow is what was lost
Did fatty tumors and bad teeth revoke your place in the family?
I like you, old girl, so much better than a yappy younger dog
But so many like you end up here, in the saddest wing of the shelter
I must see the world with different eyes
How do you put an age limit on a loyal, spunky companion?

No worries, pretty girl, you'll again be someone's faithful companion
And this time to one as faithful as you, never again to be lost
You'll be cherished and know love until the final close of your eyes
However long or short that may be, we're your last family
I promise a soft bed, a place on the couch, affection, and treats—a true shelter
Befitting such a happy, loveable dog

A dog is the most forgiving, resilient companion
Even in the shelter, when all comfort and hope seem lost
Their eyes alight with joy, trust, and devotion when they recognize they again have a family

The Cat's Out of the Bag

Rosemary Nissen-Wade

She's sitting on the chair next to mine,
demanding bits of my breakfast toast.
She stares at me and cries, she is so
desperate, she wants to tell me,
for just this treat; she is owed.
Her person (me) keeps her starving.

Earlier, after her own breakfast,
she accompanied me back to bed.

She spooned with me, settling her tiny back
into my chest, as I arced around her,
stroking her tummy and throat
while she stretched and purred.

She is my boss lady, and I'm hers.
We've made our negotiations.

There are matters on which
we renegotiate daily. We work it out.
E.g. she will use the cat door, reluctantly, if
I keep ignoring requests to open others.

But I'd like to see me try to keep her
in a bag! There would be ructions.

She would scream at me and claw,
scrabbling fiercely, the way she used to do
at the carpet outside the bedroom door
when I shut her out ... before I surrendered.

New Neighbors

Delaina J. Miller

Out from the cedar tree,
wings stretched wide,
our new neighbors build
their home in eaves of mine.
Beak load by beak load,
the sides of the roost form.
Despite the roof
that shelters us both,
the mighty Wren
places a giant leaf on top
to disguise his one-room shack.
Carpeted wall to wall
with cedar fresh needles
the newly settled home
is a cat-proof mansion.
We try to be good neighbors.
We don't ask them to water
when we are away,
and we all keep watch
of each other's doorways.

Not Fulfilling Their Obligations: A Partially Found Poem

Helen Patrice

Bikini Atoll vaporised
(just like my heart
when you said those words).
Personal injury and unfinished business
(yes, to both).
A fair and just settlement
(would see you hog-tied
while I said my loud, outraged piece).
(It would give you)
particular awareness of the dire consequences.
Nuclear disarmament would require
(you dead).
(Lest we forget).

An Owl in Love with a Deer

Delaina J. Miller

Oh me, I'm an owl.
I sleep at night so I can follow a deer.
Don't worry, I still have my insight.
That is how I found her sheltered grace.
There was a spark full of magic,
right from the start; my heart had the wisdom

not to hesitate. I'm born with this wisdom
being an owl.
One look and I saw the magic
in her doe eyes and thought: "Hoo-hoo-hoo-hoo dear!"
A thousand winks I would miss, just to see her golden grace.
My feathers ruffle with the desire she incites.

So lucky I am to have this great insight
this intuitive wisdom
to know change has its grace.
The mysteries of life are shown to an owl
just as tenderness and tenacity are common to a deer.
Besides, her eyes cast a spell—magic

it was—truly and indeed magic.
Her agile and vigilant insight,
common in a deer,
gave her the wisdom
that something was afoot with this goofy owl.
But she showed the grace,

not to laugh as I swhoo-hoo-hoo-hoon in her grace.
Maybe, just maybe she felt some magic
for this bird-brained, Great-horned owl.
We both have the insight
and the wisdom
to know the transitions will be fierce for an owl and her deer.

But what does it matter if an owl loves a deer?
Love is grace,
and life is for wisdom.
It is passion and magic
that makes insight
and devotion true for an owl

for me, and even you. Together owl and deer
inspire insight with grace,
as they frolic in a world of magic and gentle wisdom.

Why Buy the Cow?

Leigh D.C. Spencer

So, lemme get this straight—

Women are akin to livestock
purchasable commodities
valuable only
if they've never been fucked?

Not even by you,
the prospective buyer?

Not to confuse the matter
by jumping species
but
what a pile of horse shit!

Taken literally,
a good dairy cow
costs around $1,200

Which is a slight pretty penny
to spend
on the promise of sweet, plentiful milk
unsampled

A good wife
open-air bred, moderate weight, and with strong teeth
costs significantly more
than a good dairy cow

Even more costly
and downright dangerous
should you decide to sample
free milk
at neighboring farms

And, if the milk isn't free
then you're doing a direct
dollars and cents exchange for it

Isn't there a name for that?

Traditionally, I don't recall that title
being in high demand
in the wife market either

So maybe
that's not really what you meant?

Symbolically, though
it's not much prettier a picture

When you buy the marital cow
that milk might be amazing

Like, seriously

The best fucking milk
you ever tasted

For a year or two

With glimpses of glory later

But certainly not
gracing the breakfast table
every single morning

But don't despair!

You didn't just buy the milk

If you bought the right cow
the bonus plan includes

Support
Love
Laughter
Companionship
Friendship
And just maybe, even
Children!

You know,
expanding the herd
(you may not immediately see the positive cost/value ratio, but trust me, it's there)

Also

Taking care of you when you're sick
Giving a shit when you're sad
Growing old with you
Generally making every aspect of your life
(not just the smallest section of the pie graph fuckable parts)
Better
Richer
Fuller

You'd be lucky to have a cow like that

Even/especially if her milk had been freely given
to half the damn valley
before you came along

It's all about knowing what you're getting into
Seeing real value
Not being tempted by anything on the other side
of the white picket fence
because you've already grazed there

Been there
Done that
No need to go back

Of course
none of this argument matters

Because
women are not cows

And men
worth having
know
not to make important life investment decisions
with their dicks

Think higher

Everyone knows
the way to take a bull
is by the horns

My Last Duchess

Helen Patrice

Don't be stupid,
it's not even a woman.
Three eyes, fourteen breasts, a dick, yet.
Fuckin' kids with spray cans.
I just got that fence clean,
again.
They come along at night.
It's usually words, their tags,
but some bright spark likes to paint nudes.
He's very good,
but this last one –
who does he think he is?
Picasso?
My wife put up a sign:
'Please, please don't write on our wall'.
Someone wrote 'okay' underneath.
Fuckin' kids.
This is the last of it.
I'm pulling the wall down,
putting up a hedge.
Let's see the royal bastards
paint a naked woman on that.

Favourite Monster

Rosemary Nissen-Wade

I loved you, Godzilla,
and my little boys loved you,
at the local drive-in
forty-odd years ago;
and their father as well,
who is dead now …
but you, dear Godzilla, never die,
not even when you're attacked
with gigantic versions of the sparklers
we used to wave on Guy Fawkes' Night,
all sizzling and coruscating
and bouncing off your hide.

Poor clumsy Godzilla,
not even faintly humanoid,
but lumbering and alien
and rather dumb,
so slow you came across
as the underdog.
I mean, you couldn't do anything
with grace, elegance, finesse or panache –
your special effects were creaky.
We didn't even speak the same language!
You were weird (not in a good way).
You were the big ugly. You were just wrong.

Yet there was something about you.
We felt you were misunderstood.
We blamed it on your upbringing.
We knew that somewhere within
you were really good – anyway,
we were on your side. You became
our favourite monster (even dearer
than sad, persecuted King Kong).
What a pity you couldn't win an Oscar.
You could have brandished it high,
in in-your-face triumph: 'This
is for all the misfits!'

Things that Go Bump

Leigh D.C. Spencer

I love scary movies

Zombies, ghosts, demons,
just about any flavor
of murderous monster

You can count me in!

I love dead trees
old cemeteries
and houses with windows
like Amityville

We stayed in an inn once
with a 300-year-old mirror
that belonged to Mary Todd Lincoln

I stared into it for hours
even sneaking down
in dark of midnight
in my nightgown

Never saw anything
(scarier than my own face, anyway)

I dreamed of a ghost in my house
previous owner
looking for his porn stash
(that we donated to Goodwill)

He was nice enough
even though
he disagreed with my taste in paint colors
and probably missed his porn

Lest you think my entertainment tastes
make me immune
to the ingrained fraidy catcall

Let me assure you
my back hallway
makes me twitchy nervous
after dark

And I still jump into bed
from three feet across the room
hoping against hope
that the arms
of whatever lives underneath
are shorter

Into The Mind of the Alien

Helen Patrice

Okay a beek hn hn sh
Kabeeeee hn ah drer
Wha yu doin?
A free tu hn re
Bre du okay kabee hn ra.

His voice from upstairs,
in the room we call the jumping room.
He's talking to himself,
loud, insistent,
but only if no one is there.
He's always talked to someone,
invisible to all.
I thought he was a twin in utero.
Jennifer – the girl who never was.
He's never let her go.
He has many labels,
all of them walls of a box
that sits at odd angles.
He's half in this world,
half in hers,
where words don't matter.

Launching Magic

Delaina J. Miller

Do you remember that old washing machine?
We would climb on top and pretend it was our rocket ship.
Counting down, our voices getting louder with each number
10. 9. 8. 7. 6. 5. 4. 3. 2. 1. Blastoff!
In a frenzy we began twisting the dials
that would send us to Armstrong's moon.
I never saw the stars with you.
But I remember the day the motor
sparked to life and we both jumped off,
neither of us ready to take that flight.

Since You Asked

Leigh D.C. Spencer

I was just wondering
if vampires ejaculate
and, if so,
does blood, semen,
or something else
come out?
Also, I wonder if living
near the air force base and missile plant
is helpful or detrimental
during wartime?
I think it would be bad
in the event of a nuclear assault
but likely quite helpful
during the zombie apocalypse
Did you know that most male reptiles
have two penises?
Apparently, it's such a struggle
Selecting, grabbing, and restraining the females,
the survival of their species depends on
being good to go
from either side
I guess you gotta do
what you gotta do
when flowers, candy, and Barry White on the record player
aren't available options
I think I want something

with grilled onions for dinner
That's about it
since you asked
what I was thinking

A Text from My Soul

Delaina J. Miller

Because you may not hear me
or even see me before the verb "text"
becomes obsolete
there are a few things I wish you to know.

The bullies at school are scared
same as you. It's not an excuse,
it's simply the truth. They see nowhere to turn,
so they turn on you. It's nothing to do with you.

The beauty and beast are real;
they are parts that make the whole.
Whether you are boy, girl, or someone in between,
in you there is beauty and a beast that deserves love.

Adults are not always right
as you pointed out the other night.
But their wisdom is hard fought, same as yours.
Listen, then let your soul be your guide.

Believe in yourself, and honor your life;
it is too fragile to take for granted. Find value
in all things, especially things different from you.
Diversity strengthens an enlightened mind.

Above the chatter that you hear and fear,
you own my love. Wear it as armor
to cover your chest, so the insults of bullies
fall limp, and love can grow and heal.

The Basics

Rosemary Nissen-Wade

Now that I'm old and widowed
I meet up with my kind,
and all those single ladies
are of a single mind.

All their immaculate houses
quite put mine to shame.
In Domestic Goddessry,
they're at the top of their game.

'I don't want Help', they tell me;
'It gives me something to do'.
They wait expectantly,
quite sure I'll say this too.

But I'm a weirdo poet
and live a different life.
I like my house OK
but I am not its wife.

We all get back to basics
our own ways, I suppose.
I should pay more attention
to vacuum and garden hose.

But needing something to do
that badly fills me with horror.
I have poems to write –
the dishes can wait till tomorrow.

The Meanest Thing

Leigh D.C. Spencer

My ex-husband
had a way of belittling me

Subtly
I don't suppose he was trying to be gentle
he just spoke
with a tight economy of words

So many barbs
countless
underestimations

But I will never forget
that afternoon

I was musing
about the magical universe
created in the pages of Harry Potter

Wondering
when my owl might finally arrive
and what Snape looked like naked

When I must have said aloud

"Wouldn't it be great if Hogwarts were real?"

Without looking up from his paper
he sneered

"Maybe it is and you're a Muggle."

That was the meanest thing
the Dementor
ever said to me

First Date

Helen Patrice

I am resplendent in my best
red and purple flowing clothes,
awkward in gesture and word,
too much carnelian jewellery,
not enough rose quartz cleavage.
I talk in noises,
pretending interest
in his many views.
He pours wine.
It sits in my glass,
expectant.
I do not like wine.
It is the colour of a summer pear.
I long for a fresh pear.
It smells of a teen boy's socks.
I do not long for those.
I wish to be away,
eating pears, sorting laundry,
hanging up my flowing clothes.
He invites me spearfishing.
I cannot answer without laughing,
so I blink my wide-eyed response,
Morse code and semaphore flags for
'You must be joking'.
His breath smells of socks,
as he drives me home.

He tells me he won't come in
until I want him.
He drives away,
undrunk wine bottles clinking
in the back seat.
I am safe again
in solitude,
from men who fancy themselves.

Tell it to the Empty Chair

Leigh D.C. Spencer

He doesn't let me finish
a sentence

Assumes he must know
what I mean
simple as I am

Doesn't want to go out
to a party
full of people
as simple as that

My last memories
are of his fingers
and knees

I spent so many years
talking through
the newspaper
covering all else

Delivering edicts
from behind the paper walls

I issue no comment
anymore

I wonder if you notice
I'm gone?

I finally
finished my sentence

You are talking
to an empty chair

Lazarus' Jewel Box

Helen Patrice

All his life, he'd kept the box
high on a shelf.
The box made of fine white bone.
He died.
She opened it,
after the entombment.
Antique silver, enamel,
a pigeon egg sapphire –
all the things he never gave her when alive.
She adorned herself,
felt nothing,
but a dull sludge of anger.
Beauty over the top of her rough dress.

Then He came,
brought him back to life.
Jewels back in the bone box.
He took no payment;
he brooked no argument.
He was back now,
and things would be as they were.
She took to the road.
She would hunt the man
and kill him.

Trying On Clothes
(After reading Shel Silverstein)

Helen Patrice

My mother's shoes were too big,
too pointy and weird,
with high heels that hurt and schlepped.
I couldn't fill those.
My dad's woollen waistcoat
hung on me like old bags,
with buttonholes that closed their eyes
as soon as I touched them.
I couldn't fill that.
My brother's overalls were too ugly
to be worn by a little girl
who liked wispy veils,
lacy curtains, and to be wrecked on flowered islands.
I couldn't wear those.
I wore a yellow satin dress
too big for me,
but I knew I'd grow into it:
floppy netting,
shoulder straps.
I didn't care that it came
from a dance school.
I just knew this was me:
fairy child, dancer,
glamour queen with jeans underneath.

Attic

Leigh D.C. Spencer

It's dark sometimes

Light permeates
an occasional wall crack
stirring up dust to swirl
and settle on delicate cobwebs

My old things cast
frightening shadows
so much larger
than they were in life

I worry for the things I can't find

If not here
then where?

Sit in the creaking rocking chair

Back and forth
Back and forth
Again and again

Replaying each failure
each missed chance
to do things differently
to be a different, better me

Old wood creak
sounds like voices

My mother
My lover
My own

A chorus of unanimous disappointment
endlessly, rhythmically creaking

I can't leave
but it lulls me to sleep

It's dark sometimes
Here
in my head

Cold Water

Leigh D.C. Spencer

The first time we took him to the beach
it was San Diego in winter

Dipped his chubby baby toes in the surf
and he jerked them up and away
so hard and fast
his knees ended up in his tiny nose

Not a fan of cold water then
but times change

Myriad of partially full cups
scattered in every room

My particular boy
has a narrow range
of acceptable water temperature

Three ice cubes
is just right

Four is too many
And if it touches his lips
it better be cold

The Newer Habit

Helen Patrice

Morning pills again:
one white, staving off madness,
others as support.

Clearing the debris
of dark, cold, and death,
old black wishes.

White stains black,
like blood in clear water.
Tales untold, yet.

Waterfall

Delaina J. Miller

A dark heavy sky releases
    the warmth of spring.
Ripples explode across puddles
    as droplets splash in.
A dogwood tousled
    by the wind
        sleeps no more.

Storms

Delaina J. Miller

Under a heavy grey lid
the rapid boil of spring
bubbles and dances
a wintered earth—green.

Weather Report, Outside and In

Rosemary Nissen-Wade

It's a warm autumn day outside
but overcast in the house
with the blinds all closed

against the heat,
which is not extreme.
I forget that summer has gone.

I'm listening to Rufus Wainwright
soaring on YouTube, singing
Fare Thee Well ... 'oh, fare thee well'.

I've shut my doors against
one who wants to come and rest here
after his latest hurt.

He said, 'I'm not asking for a saviour
but a friend. If it goes on past a month,
I'll just add my name to the lease'.

'Oh no you fucking won't!' I said.
Now I feel as if I'd swallowed
a mass of thick grey sludge.

He says I'm harsh. I know I'm selfish.
'Have you ever had nowhere to go?'
he asks. 'Have you ever just wanted

a quiet place with a good friend?'
No. Nevertheless.
It's a warm autumn day, outside.

The Question of Safety

Helen Patrice

Is it that time of the month again?
It can't wait?
I'll do it in the shower, shall I?
Is that a lump?
What to do?
Where's the doctor's number?
Is it normal to cry from fear?
When can the specialist see me?
Those many weeks away?
It won't grow, will it?
(I won't die, will I?)
Will the biopsy hurt?
How soon can I start fading the scar
with rosehip oil?
Benign?
Is it normal to cry from relief?
So, I missed the bullet?
Which Goddess to thank?

The Last Straw

Leigh D.C. Spencer

The last straw
Slurped
the last trace of water
from around the last ice cube
Got stuck
in a triple-thick, vanilla milkshake
Blew
big, impossible milk bubbles
filling the half empty glass
Remember when the doctors said
you wouldn't be able to drink from a straw?
It was right after they said
you'd never be able to breastfeed
or blow bubbles
or play a recorder
And then you did?
The last straw—
advice we didn't listen to
because you proved them wrong
every time
The last straw
sits comfortably
in the grove of your cleft lip

Happy Easter

Rosemary Nissen-Wade

My friend phones in crisis.
'You've got to leave it be', I say.
'You can't sustain these shocks.
She's an adult now.'

'Yes', she says,
'And it cuts both ways.
If the homeless team find her,
they can't even tell me she's safe
unless she gives permission,
because she's thirty-four'.

That surprises me.
I thought the soft-faced girl
was about nineteen –
that childish gaze,
and her behaviour ...

The story this time:
the refuge kicked her out
because she got in a fight,
and the mental health clinic's full.
She's got no money, and
she's out of her medication.
She's borrowed a phone
to call her mum
from some woman in the park.

'I don't even know
if she's telling me the truth,
or how confused she might be',
her mother says.

'But I've worked out the pattern.
It's intermittent. Happens
at Christmas and Easter'.
'When did it start?' I ask.
'She was thirteen, it was after
her father's suicide'.

Her other daughter's visiting
to use her mum's computer,
and she has things to say:
'You never helped me either.
You've got to go and look for her.
You're not a proper mother'.

I know the years of care,
the returns in violent abuse.
'That's all you need', I say.
'Tell her that's the past.
Tell her to back off'.

'Oh, she's worried about her sister.
But I can't go. The lawn-mowing man
threw up a stone, and smashed
the back window of my car.
I can't go anywhere'.

Meanwhile her son with Asperger's
shuts the door of his room,
'To keep the dramas out'.

'I'm shaking and I want to vomit',
says my friend.

Before It Is Too Late

Delaina J. Miller

I'd like to make amends
      to all living things
      to the rivers and trees
      to the sky and the glens.
I offer a sincere apology
      for thoughtless words
      for neglectful deeds
      for the blind spots outside of me.
I seek mercy
      for dalliances left in disarray
      for excuses left to hold the blame
      for moments squandered in fury.
I ask for the grace
      to sing and dance as I please
      to strengthen life with poetry
      to offer diversity as commonplace.
All before it is too late.

The Poet Dreams of Dreams

Helen Patrice

The death hour,
and the last shred of you is gone.
You were hungry enough for me
the night before,
jealous of the time I spent away
from you, the rumpled rumble bed,
the sweating tumble we have together.
Last night you took me with delicate savagery,
eating me up like a hot cake.
Four in the morning, and you're done.
Another moment with me is too much.
You leave by the door,
by any open window,
the chimney flue if you could.
Only when drugged can you stay with me
till a good hour of the day.
It's a sick relationship,
we both know it:
you don't exist without me,
I can't live without you.
Oh sleep, come back as a lover
ready to see it through.

Since You Left

Rosemary Nissen-Wade

Life goes on, and that's the trouble.
You never saw the four new pictures on the wall,
the ones I love the most. You never met
all the new friends I've made these last eighteen months,
and the new next-door neighbour. I know
you could not have imagined the various new
directions I'd take, the old I would abandon.

You must have thought I'd stay
right where you left me – but stuff keeps happening,
and even the cats have made their adjustments.
We have different routines now, becoming habits,
new, unexpected ways of doing our lives.
Who ever thought I'd be so independent?
You, perhaps – stepping back and allowing for it.

You told me I could do it, and I do.
You, my greatest cheerleader, had no doubt.
But me, I seldom thought beyond your end.
It was getting us both through those hard days
that occupied me then. I forgot
that laughter could come again, and books
I'd love to read, and new poems.

And it's all good, as they say. Except when it's not.
I have so much abundant love in my life,
I should be ashamed of ever complaining. And yet
you are not here and never will be again in this life.
Don't tell me you're still with me in spirit! I know,
but it isn't the same. It's ordinary you I want to talk to
about the cats and pictures and books; that you I want to hug.

Since you left, I do this crazy thing.
I talk to you in my head. When I'm alone, I do it
out loud, and the cats understand, or at least don't question.
But it's you who have stayed where you were
when we said goodbye. You do not accompany me
on the rest of this journey; I'm going it alone.
And it sucks, do you hear me? It fucking sucks!

The Grim

Delaina J. Miller

There is a monster under my bed,
and it wants to swallow me whole
into an abyss
so dark, there is no light
for shadows to resemble your ghost.

So dark I choke
on the thick, dry void
of nothingness your death left behind.
No evidence of anything
except the raging pain
of my loss.

With news of another child's death,
memories haunt me
of how I could not save you.
There is a monster under my bed,
and it wants to swallow me whole.

Arranging After-Care
(after reading Cesar Vallejo)

Helen Patrice

I will die in Belgrave, sky and me sunny enough
while waiting for Puffing Billy.
I will fall onto the tracks – one awkward step –
on a Tuesday in autumn.

It will be a Tuesday
because that's my day off from the world,
and I know it already
the way I know how people look as babies,
as adults, as crones, just by staring long enough.

Helen is dead, those who are left will say.
Tch, a shame, because her next book would have been the one.
They will shuffle their collections
like tarot cards,

make a spread of them to divine their own ends.
They will say how they loved me,
as they count the cost of flowers for the funeral.

Remembering the Dead

Rosemary Nissen-Wade

It's the night of Samhain
here in the southern
half of the world.

I find photos
of my dear dead,
going through old albums.

Two were my mother's,
which I inherited; the rest
cover most of my life ...

most of my loves –
but there are two faces missing.
I scrabble through shelves and drawers.

A whole album, I realise
has been mislaid.
The big one with the red cover.

In that, my children were little
and there were many shots
of their handsome father

(my second husband,
the one I had the longest,
who died in January '95).

It was the only place I kept
pictures of him. But he was a friend
and should be honoured.

And my beautiful Nana,
who died when I was four –
where is she?

She hated being photographed.
So the family had only one:
official, serious, in her nurse's uniform.

I've put my copy somewhere safe.
Too safe, and now I can't
discover the hiding-place.

Eventually I call it a day –
late into the night – and go to bed
after finally casting circle.

I tell the Listeners
what I choose to discard
at this time, from my life,

and what I choose
to bring in. (Life, and all
its varied memories.)

Then I dream all night
of old homes, old dramas,
ghosts who demand their due.

When I wake, I see
it rained while I slept; the sky
is still grey, the sun

struggles through cloud,
and Samhain leaves me a task:
write the stories.

Anti-Elegy

Rosemary Nissen-Wade

'Guess who died?' I said. 'It was on Facebook.
Oh, a week or so ago. The person who posted it
described him as kind!' [Meaningful pause.] 'And humble!'
We raised high eyebrows at each other.

'You know', I said, 'I kept bumping into him
all over town, that last week before he died.
Not to speak to, though. That is, I chose not;
pretended I didn't see him. Which I still don't regret'.

'She was a lovely woman', said my friend.
'She was', I agreed, and we fell silent, remembering
his wife, whom we loved … her death nine years ago … .
'Well – I hope he worked out his karma', I said.

You Heard He Was Dead

Helen Patrice

You heard he was dead,
and said nothing out loud,
but you and your friend said plenty,
plenty!
without words.
Last Wednesday, outside Woolworths,
you said a shitload
in looks
as frozen foods went out the door,
and you both thought of hot foods
from the chicken place down the road.
You liked his wife,
and I do too now,
because I trust your judgment
in the same way I don't trust ASIO.
You both said plenty
into the loud street,
as silence pecked between you,
and those chickens punched on
to open mouths.

The Monster Collective

Leigh D.C. Spencer

Short man
dark hair
iconic mustache

About as un-Aryan
as could be
shouting charismatic ideals

Blame the monsters!

Collectively

Jew
Gypsy
Homosexual
Cripple

Give hatred a face
many faces
while somehow stripping humanity

Humans become titles
only
real as the yellow felt stars on their chests

Badges
were for children
playing at cops and robbers

But who are the good guys now?

We are!

Representing
an entire proud nation
humiliated
awaiting
returning glory days
when the evil is
exterminated
We are!
merely cutting out a cancer
so the rest may heal

But who are the monsters?

They are!

Us?

The millions dying in camps
scapegoats
butchered
to benefit a broken country

No.

It's him!

History's pointing finger says so

Little man
un-Aryan
iconic mustache

Big chip on his shoulder
that looks suspiciously like
a bar of soap
or pile of gold teeth

But it's not him
either

He was a pile of loud words
dust cloud
kicked up by soldiers' feet

Shrouding
humanity
compassion
decency

As if his words had more meaning
than what their eyes could see
hearts could feel

The fabricated vilified
took up their felt badges
as accolades
rather than turn on the master

Turn on the light
Turn up the gas

Who? Us?

We were

just following orders
saluted from small, lily-white hands

He left the blood to you

True badge
never to be unstained
of the monster collective

The Death of Poverty

Delaina J. Miller

Rulers have come and gone
who worshipped the way
you brought the poor to their knees.
So many tears shed in your name.

You taught us well,
with bloated bellies
hung on tiny brittle bones
to look with our eyes
and open our hearts.

Now that you have passed
I cannot honestly say I'm sad.
In fact for you, I hope
there is no Resurrection Day.

How I Miss Those Years

Helen Patrice

I was never lonely, those years on my own.
Echoing cold house a thrilling ice skating rink,
after dancing for three body-loving hours
to women who worshipped their bodies and souls.
I never hated in those still, frozen nights,
for I had two undemanding cats as hip holsters,
and a mattress that caressed me.
I never cried upon waking,
for the grey back fence was a sight to behold,
and winter sunlight was the strongest of all.

Strength Discovered

Leigh D.C. Spencer

It's not like it was some foreign land
Awaiting a flag

Or even like a buried treasure

I was the only one
hiding it

Although
that's also not entirely true
(neither is anything else)

You suspected it was there first

It scared us both so
that you handed me the mortar
of all our daily fears
and I dutifully troweled it over
until no one would ever suspect
it existed at all

Least of all me
seeing only this perfectly crafted edifice
(artifice)

But then
there is was

Maybe a hairline crack
started the first time I thought
I could run
I could turn left instead of right home
I could be gone

And even if you noticed,
you would wait until you finished reading the paper
cover to cover
before looking for me

On Sunday
I could make it halfway to China
if I were so inclined

You said the most hateful things then

I picked up our trowel
and you were satisfied
to see me back at work

But this time
I chipped the façade away

For the better part of two years
bit by bit

Each fortified fear
Each spackled doubt

I fully expected that when it all was gone
there would just be nothing
that I could just cease to be

So beaten down then
it was a comfort, really

Like your easy chair
paper spread from arm to arm

And me
thinking of China

When the last bit chipped away
there was so much more than nothing

There was me

When I asked for a divorce
from the other side of the newspaper

Didn't you feel it coming?

The Traveller

Rosemary Nissen-Wade

On the voyage
he falls asleep
and dreams of nothing.

The windows are dark;
they might be traversing
land or ocean.

His mind reminds him
it is really empty space out there
but he can't fathom it.

It does not seem to be a mistake
when he is woken and told
they are flying toward the sun.

He wanted to prove
something ... he's uncertain what,
but this would surely serve.

To go out in the proverbial
blaze of glory ...
but they veer, pass unharmed, and go on.

Passage

Delaina J. Miller

Oh, what a ride. A full whirlwind!
Our journey together.
Compass in hand we traverse
prairie fields, desert hills,
even gardens of the world.
Side by side we wiggle through
retaining walls to define our married life.
One decade becoming two
our knot finally recognized.

From the airplane window we watch
the earth move and we feel change.
A virgin voyage some might say,
though we return each year
it feels different this time.
Open eyes and arms wait to pull us in,
pull us close to avow our love
to celebrate
the completion of us.

Solo in San Francisco

Leigh D.C. Spencer

Business trip
my first

I don't travel well alone

The shuttle from the airport wound through
"bad" neighborhoods
graffiti, garbage, and disrepair

It reminded me of New York
with better weather

I've had some great times there
in the Big Apple
though the city itself
always scares me to death
and I've never been alone

I wondered
where they put me up

Up was sure on the right track

Up, up, and up we climbed
until looking out the window was like
looking over the car of a roller coaster

How are the streets even built so steep?

Looking over the top of a hill
is like looking at a drop off

Take a leap of faith

Miracles answered
the street continues

But we've stopped
at the very top
roller coaster car luxuriously stuck
at the Intercontinental Mark Hopkins

I'm a shy VIP
thinking I don't belong here
so I tip too much
before I plop right in the middle
of the plush kingsize bed
all for me

The work events go quickly
so I find myself on my own in China Town

I take a million pictures
eat a bean paste bun as large as my head

Souvenirs for the family
a collection of old coins
an Alcatraz shot glass
a combination soup spoon and training chopsticks
a jade unicorn (for me)
mission accomplished

Wheeze with pride over
not dying on my walk back

Up way up
those crazy streets

Tall narrow houses
beautiful and surreal
painted in pastels
packed so close together

Is huddling how they earned
earthquake survivor status?

I contemplate Ghiradelli Square
romantic pathetic dinner for one
or for me and the sea lions, at least
at Pier 39

I know my husband
my adventurer
will be disappointed
by all the sights I've missed

But I've seen them before
and the sun is setting

Back in the fancy room
I open the window
turn up the heat

It's excessive
but I love the sound of the trolley cars

Rush to the window
humming the Rice-a-Roni tune
every time I hear the bell

This is my way
enjoying (and I do!)
San Francisco—solo

When I Went Back to Melbourne

Rosemary Nissen-Wade

When I went back to Melbourne,
I was surprised by trees
greening the railway embankments
and city streets.

The wide, sunlit Yarra shone
under new bridges and old.

Then I strolled around Pascoe Vale,
delighted by roses –
thick, old bushes, well established.

How had I forgotten them
in the intervening years?

My nearest family and oldest friends
live in Melbourne. Good to spend time
with them. Good to see them happy.

'I'm afraid you'll move back',
said a friend from here.

I texted her from the midst of Melbourne traffic,
as I snuggled into a shawl against the cold
(at the beginning of summer).
'Not a chance', I said.

Still, it's nice to visit.

Dirt Roads and Forgotten Highways

Delaina J. Miller

She squeals, "Road Trip!"
Steering off the fancy, paved,
toll road we veer onto a path
few still travel.

Dark tar stretches
like veins for miles and miles.
The tires thump a baseline
we can sing a melody to.

Abandoned mills, family farms,
and wooden fences garnish
the old roads the map marks
as thin, black trails.

Narrow two-lane roads
with double yellow lines.
No fast lane
only 'No Passing' signs

until the curves straighten
and the hills flatten. Enjoy
the view. Watch the hawks
ride the currents,

and the haystacks blur
against tender grasses.
In still ponds
the sky reflects.

Today we escape
the hustle—the bustle
back to basics
a halcyon country drive.

Camping in the Rain

Leigh D.C. Spencer

Damn the forecast!
We're heading up the mountain

Car packed
and too much scheduling
to be deterred by a little rain

But what about by a whole fucking lot of rain?

Rain that sees your waterproof tent
as a personal challenge

It's ARIZONA

You know
the ARID ZONE

So this really can't
last
much
longer

Night one and we woke up
to two inches of water
on the floor of the tent

I wanted to admit defeat
but, as cummings noted,
the world was mud-luscious
and the swamp creatures replacing our children
were so very happy

We women
compromised

Decided stronger tarps
were the way to go

If you can't beat Mother Nature
you can hide from her
for about $30 worth of plastic and twine
from the Target
45 minutes down the mountain

We drank hot Starbucks coffee
laughed and listened to the radio
my best friend and I
in the front of her formerly white van

The kids
(so much smaller then)
Snoozed
in their slowly drying row of carseats

Back up the mountain
to another half day
trapped in our shelter
soaked to the bone

We finally admitted defeat
broke camp early
packed up every last soggy bundle
every drowned lantern
every sopping sleeping bag

Retreated
back down the mountain

All the while
enjoying the scenic views
on the long
warm
sunny
drive home

City of Fountains

Delaina J. Miller

Every winter they turn off
not to become frothy mounds of fluffed ice.
Fountain Day, a community sign of spring
when all the fountains come to life again.

Waters leap high in the air
or flow, rippled cascades.
On Opening Day the fountains gush Royal Blue.
For Breast Cancer Week,
fountains burst pink.

There are mermaids and warriors,
delicate nudes, even a muse.
Memorials to Nichols and Bloch
and firefighters too.

The City of Fountains
falls short only of Rome.
With bubbling gurgles for children to play
the fountains are art in wet sprays.
Just a few of the reasons to call
Kansas City home.

Colour

Rosemary Nissen-Wade

In Peru
the blue of his eyes
had the women twittering.
'So handsome' they told me.
(I already knew.)

I, of course, was gazing
(discreetly) into
the deep brown eyes
of slim, black-haired men
with knife-edge cheekbones.

In Bali
the locals feasted their eyes
on our fair-faced, fair-haired boys
(they were pre-schoolers then)
with clucks of admiring joy.

Their father and I
couldn't pull our gaze
from the quick, dark local children,
their golden skin, black hair
and bright black, dazzling eyes.

She Is

Rosemary Nissen-Wade

She is on the beach, picking up stones.
She bends to examine marks and colours.
It's a warm autumn day, but very windy.
Her little carry bag is blown sideways
despite the weight of stones and her thongs*.
(She likes the feeling of sand in her toes.)

'I'm going to paddle my feet in the water',
she says to her friend. Her friend comes too.
'Careful', she adds, her friend being a stranger
to this beach, 'The ocean plays tricks. It chases you:
entices you in too far, then pounces'.
Sure enough, the tide draws way back, and waits.

They stay on the edge. When at last it returns
with a sudden surge, it catches them only
up to their ankles. They sample it again,
spreading over their feet, which drink it
through soles, through skin;
then they retreat up the warm, firm sand.

She throws her arms wide, crying out,
her face lifted up to the sky. The sky is full
of dancing clouds. Her friend also dances.
Finally they rest on the wooden bench
overlooking the vista: sand, surf and sky.
'We've got plenty of time', they agree.

*Note to Americans: "thongs" is the Aussie term for what you call flip-flops.

Unstill Life
(with Dogs)

Leigh D.C. Spencer

I've never wondered
what I'd look like
missing an ear
Hair tucked behind
single earring
gold or silver
always a lizard
hanging on
I'd be smiling
usually
Real or frantic
but posed
for posterity
since I never seem to catch myself
unawares
No wavy lines
like wind through a cornfield
No flowers in my hair
No monkey on my shoulder
No peripherally peering pipes
(that may or may not be pipes at all)
Representation
without speculation
on what any of it means
My smile
My graying hair

My purple glasses
My dogs
Wagging and waging
to join me in the frame
no gallery will see
Motion and emotion
Documented not captured
Comfortable
in the family album
My unstill life

A Photomontage of Me

Delaina J. Miller

Scissors and glue,
maybe a canvas or two.
The self cannot be seen
without a montage of all things.
I think Hannah Höch* believed this as true.

Industry and war,
though these might be one and the same.

Baby dolls and childish things,
for me it was Mrs. Beasley and sock monkeys.

Bicycle rides in the middle of the night
when a nine-year-old's dreams would wake
her from sleep to fret about bumps in the night
and men with hairy chins. Never once thinking
she put herself in harm's way.

The suffocating silence to discover
being different is not all it is cracked up to be.
The ill-fitting mask I wore made it hard to see
the worth of me. Charlie had his angels
but what to make of me?

I am more like Hannah Höch's *The Beautiful Girl*,
a cyborg of bits and bobs cut out and removed
from an origin or place. Redesigned by another
defined and explained by a society. Always looking
for the right gallery wall to swing from.

Hannah Hoch: a German Dada artist, one of the originators of photomontage.

Passion, Madness, Orchids

Helen Patrice

Those sexual flowers,
petals opening to hearts of crimson,
gave the women flames
they found nowhere else.
A society of overheated dames,
urging their husbands out at night –
Go, destroy her orchids.
The geranium group,
the rose growers
were more polite.

I grew no orchids,
my heartsblood lay in words.
I did not belong.
The red arteries and throbbing pulses
repelled me, though I didn't know why.

Of that age now,
I understand wildness,
as I browse orchid catalogues.

A Picture Paints a Thousand Words

Delaina J. Miller

The moon hangs high,
and the slumbering sun flips over
smiling at Earth's other side.
There's no time to waste,
the train's on time and we are late.
Grab your bag;
don't hesitate.
Just over there the sun swims
in a crystal lake.
Tomorrow lies ahead,
and my love won't end.
Your dreams await
beyond the garden gate
where you can ride the moon
and kiss the stars.
It doesn't all make sense, that's true
but dreams rarely do.

If I were Writing in Sanskrit

Rosemary Nissen-Wade

I'd make curlicues and flourishes.
It would sound aloud
quite different from English. If.

My Mum said she topped the class
in Sanskrit; showed me old notebooks
in her schoolgirl script.

Poor little Anglo-Indian girl,
she didn't want to be mixed,
liked to be thought Colonial.

Me, I look white, but I'd have liked
long black hair, dark eyes,
and a smooth brown skin.

Product of my locality and time,
I disapprove of Colonial,
and I sometimes think

I'd like to have learned to write Sanskrit
in a schoolyard under banyan trees
in Puri in Orissa, long ago …

Ready to Go

Leigh D.C. Spencer

Technology
has expanded the world
to the point where
no one lives and dies
in their hometown anymore

It's good, I think

Usually

But I remember being a kid
when Sunday dinners
didn't exist, except
at my grandparents' house

Spring meant
veal burgers on the grill
and no less than five salads
my grandmother made by hand

Summer was pizza
on the living room floor
badminton and backgammon
on blankets in the big backyard

Winter was a bucket of ribs
from Chicken Delight around the corner
unspoken eating contests
Norman and Greg would have
leaving mammoth graveyards behind
on greasy paper plates
(Skinny Norman NEVER won)

No need for hasty update phone calls
or email yet uninvented

We'll just see you on Sunday!

Until I boarded the plane
for college
across the country
because people can do that now
I was ready to go!

And then
I never came back

Except to cram two years' worth of Sunday dinners
into five days at Thanksgiving

My kids have no idea
what every Sunday dinner feels like
beyond us four

When there is so much badminton
laughter and dizziness
you fall asleep in the grass
counting grey puffs
on the endlessly high pussy willow
Wake up to mason jars of lightning bugs
while grandpa flips the burgers

This year
the offer came
for my twelve-year-old son

His grandparents invited him
to spend two whole weeks with them
sleepaway camp equivalent
of the magic I had every Sunday

He'll board the plane
(if I let go of his hand)
and walk himself through
his own future nostalgias

But he WILL come back
at least this time

It doesn't matter now
beautiful memories you leave behind
because you can VISIT them!
Technology
providing my first taste
of what's to come
when he's really
ready to go

The Last Straw Poem

Rosemary Nissen-Wade

We didn't know it would be the last,
hadn't exactly planned it that way.
When it was finished, we thought it
as decorative as the rest,
as well-constructed.

But then those poets down the road
built the first wooden one.
Everything was instantly different.
The rules had completely changed.
(Nice it was, of balsa, light and graceful.)

Then, of course, everyone tried.
The timber used grew thicker.
This didn't always produce
the most tractable results,
but they were lasting.

In time came the bold
experiments in metal.
And now a new departure
thanks to the internet:
cyber-poems, lighter than air.

I came across it the other day,
that last straw poem,
forgotten in a cupboard.
I wondered at its primitive ephemerality –
but it was sweetly woven.

In Kitchens All Over Suburbia

Helen Patrice

Your life will be soup,
some days.
Carrots, lumps of pumpkin,
green beans
swirling around the hard gristle
of a bone.
You'll wonder why you ever started cooking,
with two toddlers barking
at your legs,
the house looking
at you with sad neglect.
You wanted this minestrone of family,
thinking it was chicken broth
to heal all hurts.
Your wounds run too deep
for garlic and comfrey to salve.
Your days will boil and congeal
and nourish everyone but you.
You'll be left with the bone,
white and grim on the kitchen bench.
You'll realise you forgot to add parsley
for extra iron.
And you'll think it was all worth it,
perhaps.

Cinquain for Phillip

Rosemary Nissen-Wade

Forget
global warming.
You cook dates in curry!
Now I know civilisation
is doomed.

Meeting In Coles

Rosemary Nissen-Wade

Her chair looks heavy and solid,
though it glides quietly
through the Pension Day crowds.
'Does this make life easier?' I ask.

'Yes, and quicker.
If I walk, even with the trolley,
it can take hours.
Anyway, how are you?'

'Not too bad', I say,
'All things considered'.
She laughs and splutters. 'Yes,
that about says it here, too'.

A sweep of her arm takes in
the chair and the pile of shopping.
She's trying to help her husband
load it on the checkout tray.

The store radio doesn't just hum;
it roars. Trolleys around us clatter.
A child squeals incessantly.
The fluorescents glare.

'Take that kid home',
she says *sotto voce*, and to me,
'Don't you think that radio noise
is much too loud? I keep telling them'.

The one trouble with the chair,
she confides, is it won't fit in the car.
'We have to take the maxi taxi, and
they won't park outside our house.

'Poor old Patrick has to take
all the shopping across the road
and then up our front steps'. How old
is Patrick now, I wonder. I don't enquire.

'Are you online?' I ask. 'Think about
Coles' delivery service. I used to use it
when Andrew was alive'. My mind goes back
to hauling his walker in and out of the car.

'I will!' she promises, and I don't add,
'Then you'll be that little bit more
house-bound'. I know, and she knows,
there are no easy choices.

Sweetness Settled

Leigh D.C. Spencer

The tea is bitter

I like it dark
but this brew stings my tongue

The warmth still soothes
steam eases my breathing

So I am thankful overall
to relax into the last sips

But there
suddenly
a sweetness almost cloying

Honey
forgotten

Settled
at the bottom of the cup

Should I have stirred it up
to sweeten the whole journey?

Or be thankful
overall
to appreciate all I had
while savoring the last surprise
of settled sweetness?

Night Poem

Rosemary Nissen-Wade

'Write a night poem',
came the instruction,
and at once I went blank.
I won't say my mind went blank;
no, it was full of invention.

I started a poem about
black velvet skies
and diamond stars,
but I couldn't extend it
past that hackneyed image.

I thought of writing how nights
are lonely now without you –
but the fact is, although true,
that's only part of the story. I
am one who likes aloneness.

I planned fantastical,
lurid words to conjure up
magickal tales of the night,
perhaps without much meaning.
They seemed too silly.

I picked up my book instead,
settled against my pillows,
sipped my cocoa and patted my cat,
as I like to do at night. But you can't
make a poem out of that.

The Secret's in the Sauce

Leigh D.C. Spencer

Tough skins split
in the boiling water

Pink innards puff
through the scar lines

Supposedly
that sound
is just a final release of steam

But I like to think
I hear my victims
screaming

One at a time

Until all that remains
is a tide of red foam
rhythmic, gurgling bubbles

Stir through
looking for survivors

Wood comes back
awash in crimson

Washed thus
never to be clean again

Stained weapon
now particularly purposed
year after bloody year

You smell fragrant orange and clove
a chunk of crisp walnut to finish

Cheery cranberry color
shimmering
like a bowlful of delicious rubies
next to the comparably peaceful turkey
I could give you the recipe
but it will never be the same

So much more
than the sum of raw ingredients

The sadism of the chef
is the secret of the sauce

That Smell

Rosemary Nissen-Wade

That smell when I opened the cupboard tonight
linked me back to my past and my further past.
I am a young mother in her kitchen.
I am a child in my own mother's kitchen.
I was making myself a cup of cocoa
to take with me to my bed, to help me sleep.

The night was fading at last from hot to warm.
The cupboard released aromas: tea, coffee,
sugar, and the cocoa's chocolatey waft.
It was all subtle. You could include paper –
that fine, fresh scent of clean paper, barely there.
All of these scents together were faint and light.

But they were enough. Enough to connect me
back to selves who I used to be. The same food –
no, the same drink – unchanged through generations
of my family, and other families
in English-speaking homes where cocoa is drunk,
throughout the world, becomes link, becomes message.

Or where tea is drunk, or coffee. Where there is
a cupboard, kitchen cupboard, with wooden doors.
Some household where all the habits, all the smells
combine in a continuous way of life,
and cocoa made with milk and drunk with sugar
is what you have at bedtime to help you sleep.

A message from the past, from my ancestors!
And from my past selves to the me I am now.
It is a good message. It has no content
except itself, its existence. The message
is the message. 'Continuity', it says,
and, 'Lineage'. And it seems to say, 'Comfort'.

Peanut Butter and Jelly

Leigh D.C. Spencer

I was dreaming
about mutton and fry bread

They still serve that
in places on the reservation
through New Mexico
or maybe Utah?

I don't even remember
where we were that trip

Except that we were hungry
and it was the middle of nowhere

Gas station

Truly last stop
maybe forever
and fifteen minutes before closing

My older son and I ran in
scouring the scant aisles
like we were stalking prey
in the first world

We captured
a loaf of soft white bread
a jar of creamy, no-name peanut butter
and two jars of strawberry preserves

(one that my son broke in his hunting haste
and the one that we took with us,
not needing to be cleaned up
now ten minutes before closing)

I don't know why we had a plastic butter knife
in the glove compartment

I do know those sandwiches were delicious
sitting on the tailgate with my family
Eating and laughing
as a glorious sunset
painted the middle of nowhere

Starts

Delaina J. Miller

Spring a closer of sorts,
heralding winter's end
with robin trills and daffodils.
While dormant yellows brighten
to tiny pods of green.
Lusterless frost turns to dew,
buds become blooms.

From the mound
a pitch is thrown
Crack!
Cheers rain down
a diamond field.
Pop flies and Cracker Jacks;
      it's Opening Day!

Elegy for DeAnza

Leigh D.C. Spencer

So many summer Saturday nights
we would pack up our lawn chairs
load the backseat with blankets and stuffed animals
grab the bucket of chicken

Family size

Grocery bag full of homemade popcorn
Big Gulp drink refill

Coordinate the caravan
so we could all be parked
in the same row
at the DeAnza Drive-in

Summer nights in Tucson
are more forgiving than days
and the kids could run around
play
make noise
as long as they didn't go past
our line of cars
four or five deep

First show was at 8 pm
we'd pick a kids' feature

Then at 10 pm,
we'd circle the lot until the kids were asleep
and choose another screen

Raunchy comedies or
over-the-top horror movies
were the undisputed BEST
for the drive-in experience

I'm still laughing over
our brilliant commentary track
during Drag Me to Hell
now five summers ago
We never knew that was your last year

1951-2009

A beautiful life
that brought so many happy times
with family and friends

It's hard to look forward to summer the same way
now that you're gone

Reduced
to (another) pricey parking lot

I've heard it said
that one of your screens was saved
and that
just maybe
they will try to bring you back some day

I know

It's just a movie screen
from a beat-up, old theatre
from the good old days
and not the Shroud of Turin

But I don't need the second coming
just the second feature
and for this
I pray

Baby Longs to Be Admiral

Helen Patrice

Little fluffy wedge-head lifts her face.
'Oh great mysterious thing
of tiny metal cross-hairs,
open thyself that I may exit
and claw the fence.
Oh magic portal,
my eyes command thee open.
The sky disk calls me
to glow in its rays'.
She cannot fathom why
doors and walls do not slide open,
Star Trek whooshing style,
as she telepathically sends her thoughts.
One day, one day,
she will have the captain's chair,
and she will command the house.

Alternate Realities

Rosemary Nissen-Wade

When my sons were young
and annoying,
I'd stomp around the house
crying, in that harsh, metallic voice:
'EX-TERM-IN-ATE! EX-TERM-IN-ATE!'
They didn't laugh.
(Just rolled their eyes and scoffed.)

Now those boys are long ago
grown and gone.
I have the house all to myself
except for my pets.
The cats are sweet;
they never get jealous
when I mother my dragons.

My Knight in Teddy Bear PJs

Delaina J. Miller

He announces
his name is Frodo,
though I can stay Aunt Delaina.
Wielding a sword in the air,
he shouts,
"Look out
behind you."
With practiced moves
and confidence
he skillfully rescues me,
time and time again,
from a peril only he can see.
I thank him
though he does not understand
he frees my heart
with his innocent grin.

Pop Culture on Loan

Delaina J. Miller

This is not *The Philosophy of Andy Warhol*
or a *Zombie Apocalypse*.
Card catalogues, a thing of the past
you won't need to crack *The Da Vinci Code*
to find *Where the Girls Are*
or understand what *Feminism and Pop Culture*
are about. You might try *The Hunger Games*
to understand all that, but don't read it at *Twilight*
with the lights off, or *Alone*.
If music is more your thing
there is *High Fidelity*
though our LPs are now CDs and MP3s.
You'll need a card to check out *Steve Jobs*,
but a membership to *Fight Club*
is not required. We won't even mind
when you use a PC to play *Candy Crush*.
Remember in this *Fast Food Nation*
of *Freakonomics*
and *Bossy Pants*
there are always *The Perks of Being a Wallflower*
at your public library. The magic we want to see in the stacks
is *Harry Potter the College Years*.

War Games

Rosemary Nissen-Wade

When I got my Kobo Wi-Fi
(which is now obsolete and dead)
it came with one hundred and one
free downloads from Gutenberg dot com –
classics, including
Homer's *Iliad*. Well!
Always wanted to read that. Felt I should.

It was the great Alexander Pope's translation,
so I thought it must be good
(forgetting I was never mad on Pope).

Every male friend who saw me reading it
seized the e-reader out of my hands,
devoured a few paragraphs,
then handed it back reluctantly, exclaiming,
'Such good stuff, isn't it?'

I must say, I didn't quite get it,
but I persevered. For several chapters.
By which time it gradually dawned –
it's a boys' book. This one fights that one,
these ones fight them. And in between
they give rousing speeches
urging each other on,
or occasionally chiding the few cowards.

They do like a bit of biffo, blokes.

Not me. I deleted Homer.

Optimist and Pessimist Attend A Fundraiser

Leigh D.C. Spencer

Optimist
assumes

the cause is just
the speakers will be inspirational
the heartstrings will be tugged
the purse strings will be loosened

Pessimist
knows

the cause is one of many and we can't help them all
the speakers will be mind-numbingly boring
the applause will be polite
the donations will be meager

Both
eat dessert first

Just in case
they're right

Signs of the Future

Delaina J. Miller

Doomsday believers
with placards and cardboard signs
that read:

The End is Near!
The End is Here!
Jesus is Coming!

The letters bold and red
carry the weight of despair,
starve the spirit,
and deny my lips Hallelujahs.

Around the corner
draped over youthful shoulders,
her sign reads,
The Future is NOW!

In that moment
past, present, and future unite.
It is now the future.
Let the signs read:

Abundance Thrives!
Gratitude Lives!
We are the saviors we need!

Comforting Myself

Rosemary Nissen-Wade

My little cat is old and ill
but so far in no pain.
Her cancer's growing slow.

When I lie down for a nap
she comes and purrs with me,
but when I start to dream
she moves away

as if she too can see
the crowding images
that seem so real.

With such a bond
between our spirits,
surely it will stretch
to keep us connected, later?

Safe Havens

Delaina J. Miller

A bunny tucks butt to trunk
under a cedar's fur,
a bristled cloak.
Green shoots grow
under a magnolia tree,
a pink and white canopy.
In a small quaint house
under large oak trees,
your love shelters me.

Doing the Usual

Rosemary Nissen-Wade

At the quiet end
of an autumn afternoon
the rain comes down
softly and steadily.

I open a shiraz,
make some conversation with the cats,
fetch my cardigan
and check the TV program.

It's almost as if you're still here.
I half-expect, any minute,
that you'll call from the bedroom
or walk from your office
to share the wine, the TV, the cats ...

This morning at my market stall
I put my clients in touch
with their dear dead.
Invariably I'm moved to tears
by the depth of love
the dead have for the living,
and my clients cry too.

I was you today, at the market,
doing the rounds of the other stalls early.
But I didn't get your abundant
bundles of fresh veggies –
not for only one.

It's BBQ chicken tonight,
to save cooking.
The cats will demand their share.
I'll give them less than they ask
(not as soft as you were)…

A nice night to be in,
as rain and evening arrive together.
Like a blanket, darkness
wraps us round.

Family Quilt

Delaina J. Miller

A constant
refreshing
tender
loud roar
of dysfunction
that functions.

Death
rips out seams,
a calico quilt
left in tatters.

Marriages,
children,
grandchildren,
nieces and nephews
patch the holes
to keep bitter cold
from settling in our hearts.

Heartaches
and triumphs together;
a golden thread
to stitch, strengthen
and bind our lives
into a definable whole

we call family.

Note to Self

Leigh D.C. Spencer

Breathe
Deeply
Look around
at the inventory of your life
It's not as cluttered and haphazard as you think
(Really!)
You'll never believe this
but you are handling things beautifully
The good surrounding you
is no accident
If you can't take credit
can you at least take the compliment?
Worry invades like a plague of locusts
but locusts have a definitive season
Uncrinkle your brow
your crops will endure
Eventually
You'll remember the bounty
Vividly
The invasion
Hardly at all
For now
Just remember to
Breathe

Tell It To the Lips

Delaina J. Miller

Say it in love's voice.
Say it in a kiss, the shooting star,
with a feather's touch
tickling inside flesh.
The alchemy of lovers' rituals.
A gentle breath, a union
of this moment
with yesterdays and tomorrows.
Speak your love
tell it to the lips
so my whole body knows.

Bitter Love Poem

Rosemary Nissen-Wade

Had a sudden flashback today.
Opening the wardrobe which now
houses my winter clothes,
for a moment I saw the ghosts
of all your garments.

The black leather jacket
with the collar just starting to go;
the maroon blazer you bought
when our marriage was new;
the yellow raincoat from Edinburgh
that matched mine, which I still have;
the fawn shorts; the grey trousers;
all your shirts and T-shirts.

I didn't keep them.
Some people need a shrine,
but not me. I didn't want
to look at them and cry.
And for all this time I didn't.
(A year and a half and a bit.)

Today, for no visible reason,
I saw them anyway,
hanging there as usual –
only it's not usual any more –
and sure enough I howled,
leaning my forehead
on the quickly-closed door
and wailing, all alone.

HOME

Leigh D.C. Spencer

Under this roof
there is safety

Protection

from the elements
but elementally more

Acceptance

Love

Strength

Walls fortified by laughter
holding in sweet
lingering aromas
of six and twelve
birthday cakes

Salty tears
for 183 scraped knees
and broken hearts
patched together
with Scooby Doo bandaids
and a kiss

It won't always be like this

Children grow

Parents grow old

Houses get sold

Let it go

Know

It was never wood and concrete
paint and tile and glass

Come to me

In sun
In storm
In laughter
In love

For as long as this heart has a beat
you will find your shelter
within

Early Morning

Helen Patrice

Pale gold sun edging into white.
Dark trees still.
Telephone lines empty of birds.
Fast flying raven.
Red roofs frosted.
Grey bitumen black with shadows.
Pink woman walking,
timing her steps,
shoes matching her tracksuit.
Cars graze the roundabout:
quick, to the main road,
to drive to work.
Lavender hills on the horizon,
quiet rain there.
Silent air sitting light.
One ginger cat, sleeping.

Love Song to an Animo Acid

Helen Patrice

With you inside me
the night is open
to black satin dreams.

With you inside me
my body unfurls
like a prayer plant.

With you inside me
my dreams are bloody
but no longer matter.

With you inside me
sleep is a lover;
we are a soft triangle.

I Love

Leigh D.C. Spencer

Day's end
when you tuck me in

Looking into your eyes
caressing beard stubble
in the calm of closing another day
together

A dog (or two) barks

A child (and a stuffed blue gorilla) will wander in soon enough

All parts
of the living dream
we put together
with our own two hands
two hearts
sealed with the mortar
of our twisted humor

If only
we weren't too tired
to make love
to sign the contract
again

Maybe tomorrow
or the tomorrow after that
or after that
or all the tomorrows we are gifted
in this delicious life

I chose

I live

I love

If I Were a Love Poem

Delaina J. Miller

I would woo you
to keep you warm all night,
dreaming of things we could do,
bodies so close
breath held tight,
nothing concealed,
denied
or untried.

I would have you wanting,
as you tasted my words on your lips.
Your radiant smile
forever held in my stanzas
your sigh—
line breaks
setting our passion
to the right pace.

Faithful to the arousal
of words you read me
again
and again,
vows of rapture,
phonetic ecstasy;
you might even share me
if I were a love poem.

Unveiling

Leigh D.C. Spencer

Did she even wear a bridal veil,
I wonder?

When she married my grandfather
in a group ceremony
in the Lodz ghetto
as a matter of propriety
so she could live with his family
when hers was taken?

Was there even a need
for that moment?

Glorious anticipation
the rosy face
of a hopeful virgin
kissing her new husband
who was just yesterday a neighbor
that she did not
and still does not
love?

They made it out
in the end

I mean
that's how I came to be
here
speculating
an unveiling that was
maybe happier

This week
they will unveil
the engraved granite slab
that seals your vault

Home now for a year

We've had this time
to roll the taste of your absence
around on our tongues
Salty, bitter, and sweet

As is the custom
our formal grieving
ends here

But where to begin?

This new day
this first step
truly without you

Unveiling
is a ceremonial term
a formality bearing
no silks
no anticipation
just a necessary reality

As before

Standing in for the rosy virgin,
my shaking finger
traces the lines
of a beautiful name
and a terrible date
etched in stone

Since I Said Yes

Delaina J. Miller

The orange cones of marriage laws
have changed from 'road closed'
to 'road work ahead.'

A crystal rainbow sparkles
from my second finger next to the sentimental
band from our fifth anniversary.

Support weeps
a sap to sweeten
bitter blows of the past.

Hearts of family and friends reveal
they are in our corner cheering us,
more than our visions dared.

White Anglo-Saxon Love

Helen Patrice

So much of our knowledge of love is rooted
in Western civilisation.
Books tell only part of the story
of our global world.
What do we know of Asian love,
Russian, Serbian, Sumerian?
Follow the love of yin-yang cosmology,
the Mandate of Heaven, Confucianism, and Daoism.
It is not enough to know the Western half
of the story.
Descend to the Underworld,
ascend to other worlds, new lives,
and find the rest of the story.

Settled

Rosemary Nissen-Wade

We settle down on the bed again after breakfast,
we three, the cats and me, all of us elderly now
and free to indulge – though they are freer than me,
and can stay here all day if they will, and in fact they will
until I give them their lunch (the small dry biscuits
that keep their teeth clean and strong) after which
they'll wander outdoors awhile, now that the weather's autumnal:
cooler than the worst heat of summer and not yet chilly winter ...

whereas I, when I finish the coffee I brought back to bed,
and finish this morning's poem, shall rise at once
to go out into the world – where, too, I am settled,
into my familiar lifestyle: the small town,
the old and new friends, the little cafés,
the trees and the nearby river.

River Ends

Delaina J. Miller

From the head it rages down;
moving earth, reflecting sky.
It pushes and shoves
in rumbles and roars.
A violent lullaby.

Swift current rushes
around that which refuses
to move. Never looking back,
never to return,
as time passes by.

At the river's end
an artist paints
a skimming dragonfly
above the placid pan
that reflects the sky.

Calling It a Day

Leigh D.C. Spencer

Thirteen hours
on my feet

Dealing with the ridiculous things
rich people care about

Like nametags
table assignments
and the crunch of the crème brulee

The Dean got drunk
slurred speech
turned all the talking points
into curves

Wallets opened anyway
so, a toast to that!

I would gladly have traded
my $100 plate of fish
(and crunchy crème brulee)
for cheap pizza and cartoons
with my non-jet-set
who don't care about nametags
or seating assignments
except for who gets to sit next to mama
on the couch

Finally
in bed that night
I said
"My god, it feels so good to be back here with you!"

My husband said he missed me too

I told him
"Honey, I love you, but just now?
I was talking to my pillow."

Future Poem
(For the Discouraged)

Rosemary Nissen-Wade

The future poem
will scintillate, startle, shock.

It will amaze, amuse,
arouse and enrage.

It won't let go of you. And you
will never be able to let it go.

The future poem will be
a miracle of poetic pleasure.

You will roll in bliss with this poem,
falling on the grass and laughing.

The future poem will whisper
in your open ear: sweet everythings.

Then it will lift you up
and shake you like a whirlwind.

The future poem will spin you
like a top, until you shriek.

When you step inside the future poem,
you will see landscapes too beautiful to bear.

Look! Look up ahead – do you see
the future poem beckoning? Keep looking.

Yes, that figure of steel and crystal,
that exotic shape, is the future poem.

It is in YOUR future. Please, take heart!
Your present poems are merely steps on the way.

Finished!

Delaina J. Miller

Standing over thirty pots of clay,
she rubs her palms together.
I have done all I can do.
Planted in neat and crooked rows.
It is up to Nature now. Let's see
how many April showers will spill
into May. And how many poems
will bloom in the hearts of strangers.

The Prompts That Started It All

In 2014, there were two different challenges during the month of April. They were NaPoWriMo and Poem A Day (PAD). Here is the list of prompts from both challenges in case you want to play "Guess the Prompt."

April 1
NaPoWriMo: Write a poem based on the quote generated from the link "Ask the Oracle" from Reb Livingston's *Bibliomancy Oracle*.
Poem A Day: Write a beginning poem or an ending poem.

April 2
NaPoWriMo: Write a non-Greco-Roman myth poem.
Poem A Day: Write a voyage poem.

April 3
NaPoWriMo: Write a simple rhyming charm poem.
Poem A Day: Write a message poem.

April 4
NaPoWriMo: Write a "lune" format poem.
Poem A Day: Write a poem with a title "Since (blank)."

April 5
NaPoWriMo: Write a "Golden Shovel" form poem.
Poem A Day: Write a discovery poem.

April 6
NaPoWriMo: Write a poem from a word list made of verbs you see happening outside your window.
Poem A Day: Write a night poem.

April 7
NaPoWriMo: Write a love poem for an inanimate object.
Poem A Day: Write a self-portrait poem.

April 8
NaPoWriMo: Write a famous poem.
Poem A Day: Write a violent poem and a peaceful poem.

April 9
NaPoWriMo: Write a poem from a random song playlist.
Poem A Day: Write a poem using the word or concept of "shelter."

April 10
NaPoWriMo: Write an advertisement poem.
Poem A Day: Write a future poem.

April 11
NaPoWriMo: Write a poem about wine and love.
Poem A Day: Make a statement. Use that statement as the title and then expand or answer the statement to create a poem.

April 12
NaPoWriMo: Write a "replacement" poem.
Poem A Day: Write a city poem.

April 13
NaPoWriMo: Write a "kenning" poem.
Poem A Day: Write an animal poem.

April 14
NaPoWriMo: Write a poem in which every line is a question except for the last line.
Poem A Day: Write a "If I Were (blank)" poem.

April 15
NaPoWriMo: Write a "terza rima" form poem.
Poem A Day: Write both a love and an anti- love poem.

April 16
NaPoWriMo: Write a ten-line poem in which each line is a lie.
Poem A Day: Write an elegy poem.

April 17
NaPoWriMo: Write a poem specifically describing something in terms using at least three senses.
Poem A Day: Write a pop culture poem.

April 18
NaPoWriMo: Write a "ruba'i" form poem.
Poem A Day: Write a weather poem.

April 19
NaPoWriMo: Write a poem from a (giving) list of seashells.
Poem A Day: Pick a color and use it in the title of your poem.

April 20
NaPoWriMo: Write a poem in the voice of a family member.
Poem A Day: Write a family poem.

April 21
NaPoWriMo: Write a "New York school" poem.
Poem A Day: Write a "back to basics" poem.

April 22
NaPoWriMo: Write a poem in which two things have a fight.
Poem A Day: Write an optimistic as well as a pessimistic poem.

April 23
NaPoWriMo: Write a poem for children.
Poem A Day: Write a location poem.

April 24
NaPoWriMo: Write a poem about masonry elements.
Poem A Day: Write a poem to the phrase "Tell it to the (blank)."

April 25
NaPoWriMo: Write a poem that uses anaphora.
Poem A Day: Write a "last straw" poem.

April 26
NaPoWriMo: Write a poem as a curtal sonnet.
Poem A Day: Write a water poem.

April 27
NaPoWriMo: Write a poem about a given photograph.
Poem A Day: Write a monster poem.

April 28
NaPoWriMo: Write a poem using words taken from a news article.
Poem A Day: Write a settled poem.

April 29
NaPoWriMo: Write a "Twenty Little Poetry Projects" poem from a given list.
Poem A Day: Write a realism poem and a magical poem.

April 30
NaPoWriMo: Write a farewell poem.
Poem A Day: Write a "calling it a day" poem.

Acknowledgements

All of the poets would like to thank Jeanie Tomanek for allowing them to use her art *Sister of the Storm* on the cover. Thanks also to Allison Pang for her design skills in creating a dynamic cover and interior for *She Too: Four Voices in (Almost) Harmony*.

About the Poet: Delaina J. Miller

Delaina Miller is a poet, publisher, sound therapist, Reiki Master, and caregiver. Delaina writes poetry because it's her favorite medium to capture snippets of the human experience. She creates Soundology as an energy health modality because she believes music is the rhythm of our soul. Other poetry books by Delaina include *She Too: Four Voices in (Almost) Harmony* and *The Unique and Sundry*. You can listen to her albums and singles from your favorite streaming platform.

About the Poet: Rosemary Nissen-Wade

Poet, memoirist. Author of several monographs and chapbooks; included in various collaborative works (such as this) and numerous magazines and anthologies over the years.

Performance poet, reviewer, editor, poetry blogger, facilitator of writers' groups on and offline. Helped start Poets Union of Australia in the late seventies. Pioneered poetry workshops in Melbourne prisons in the early eighties. Member of 'Word of Mouth' poetry theatre group, mid-eighties. Independent poetry publisher 1982-1992 (proprietor of Abalone Press and member of Pariah Press Cooperative).

Career in librarianship 1962-1980.

Reiki Master, psychic medium, Tarot reader, witch; also studied Druidry, ceremonial magic, Kabbalah.

Born and grew in Launceston, Tasmania. As an adult lived many years in Melbourne; now happily subtropical.

About the Poet: Helen Patrice

Helen Patrice is an Australian neurodiverse writer living in Naarm (Melbourne). She writes speculative and literary poetry, speculative short fiction, creative nonfiction, and memoir. She occasionally blogs at WordPress and SubStack. Her books: *A Woman of Mars, Palaentology for Beginners, She Too: Four Voice in (Almost) Harmony Three Cycles of the Moon, The Communicant and Other Stories*, and *Into Dark Woods* (forthcoming). Her recent publications include *Metonym, Pure Slush, Lady Liberty, Moss Piglet, Young Ravens, Eye to the Telescope,* and *Fairy Tale Magazine*. Helen takes part in NaNoWriMo most years and has a cache of hidden novels that are hot messes.

About the Poet: Leigh D.C. Spencer

Leigh D.C. Spencer is a writer, baker, reptile enthusiast, storyteller, aspiring middle school English teacher, and a crazy dog lady. She proudly serves on the board of F*ST! Female Storytellers, boosting the signal of female-identifying voices and fiercely supporting the notion that words have power, and everyone has a story to tell.

Leigh shares her anxious, chaotic, hilarious (sometimes on purpose), and generally wonderful life with husband Earl, sons Zac and Henry, a revolving cast of many pets, and an eclectic band of friends (real and imaginary)—all of whom she adores beyond measure.

Leigh is ... me! I am so lucky and grateful.